MULTICOOKER
ALL-IN-ONE

In the
KITCHEN

ALLISON WAGGONER

FRONT TABLE BOOKS
AN IMPRINT OF CEDAR FORT, INC.
SPRINGVILLE, UTAH

ISBN: 978-1-4621-1928-8

Published by Front Table Books, an imprint of Cedar Fort, Inc.

2373 W. 700 S., Springville, UT, 84663

Distributed by Cedar Fort, Inc., www.cedarfort.com

LIBRARY OF CONGRESS CONTROL NUMBER: 2016942332

Cover and page design by M. Shaun McMurdie

Edited by Justin Greer

Printed in the United States of America

10 9 8 7 6 5 4 3 2

For Jordon

She believed you were a superhero. As it turns out . . .
she was right. Never forget to believe in all things good.
Love, Mom

Cinnamon Brioche Bread Pudding with Orange Zest Whipped Cream

Cinnamon Brioche Bread Pudding with Orange Zest Whipped Cream

Custard

¾ cup whole milk

¾ cup heavy cream

½ cup sugar

1 teaspoon vanilla extract

1 pinch nutmeg

1 teaspoon cinnamon

3 large eggs

Bread Filling

3 ounces butter, softened

2 teaspoons sugar

2 teaspoons cinnamon

8 slices brioche, toasted until light brown

½ cup pecans, chopped

Icing

1 cup heavy cream

½ teaspoon vanilla extract

3 teaspoons orange zest

Custard
Combine the milk, heavy cream, sugar, vanilla extract, nutmeg, and 1 teaspoon of cinnamon in large bowl. Stir until the sugar is dissolved. Add the eggs and whisk until mixed completely.

Bread Filling
Mix the softened butter with sugar and cinnamon. Spread the mixture on each slice of bread. Cut the slices into 2-inch cubes, keeping 3 slices cut in half for the top if desired.

Assembly
Place the bread into the cooking pot. Top with half slices. Top with the pecans. Pour the milk mixture over the bread and press down to help the bread absorb the milk mixture. Let sit for 20 minutes.

Place cooking pot into the cooker. Lock lid in place; select High Pressure and 15 minutes cooking time. When beep sounds, turn off cooker and use a natural pressure release for 5–8 minutes until all remaining pressure is released. When valve drops, carefully remove lid. When slightly cooled, remove onto serving platter.

Icing
While cooking, whisk or beat the cream to soft peaks. Add in vanilla and orange zest.

Top the bread pudding with the whipped cream and serve warm.

Steel Cut Oats with Cinnamon, Honey, and Vanilla Bean

2 cups water

1 cup whole milk

pinch of salt

1 cup steel-cut oats

1 vanilla bean, halved and sliced lengthwise

1 cinnamon stick

1 teaspoon ground cinnamon

1 teaspoon honey

Add the water, milk, salt, oats, vanilla bean, and cinnamon stick to the cooking pot.

Lock lid in place; select High Pressure and 8 minutes cooking time. When beep sounds, turn off cooker and use a natural pressure release for 5-8 minutes until all remaining pressure is released. When valve drops, carefully remove lid. During this time, the oats will continue to cook.

Oats will continue to cook and absorb the liquid for a few minutes. If the oats still seem a little firm, put them back to pressure cook for a few minutes.

Remove the lid, then remove the vanilla bean and cinnamon stick and set aside. Stir in the ground cinnamon and honey to taste.

Add seasonal fruits to enjoy with your oats.

Steel Cut Oats with Cinnamon, Honey, and Vanilla Bean

Decadent Vanilla Bean Yogurt

Decadent Vanilla Bean Yogurt

1 gallon 2% milk

3 tablespoons powdered milk

1 vanilla bean, sliced lengthwise

½ cup yogurt with active cultures

1 tablespoon vanilla extract

You will need a kitchen thermometer for successful results.

In the cooking pot add milk, powdered milk, then scrape in vanilla bean. Set to Slow Cook function on Low setting, leaving the lid off. Use a thermometer for this process, as you need be precise when making yogurt.

Heat to 180 degrees. After reaching temperature, remove the cooking pot and let cool to 100–110 degrees. Do not let the temperature drop below 90 degrees.

Stir in the yogurt and extract until it is smooth with no lumps.

Place the lid on the cooker and lock the lid. Turn the pressure release valve to the steam position. Press the yogurt button and press start. Do not move the cooker once the function has started. The preset time is 8 hours. You can add time if you would like it to be more tart or more of a greek style of yogurt. You can time this for up to 24 hours.

Once the yogurt is ready, move to the refrigerator for up to 7 days.

Beets with Lime and Toasted Pine Nuts

Beets with Lime and Toasted Pine Nuts

1½ pounds beets, whole (similar in size, 2–3 inches in diameter)
1¼ cups water
3 tablespoons white vinegar
1 tablespoon brown sugar
1 shallot, sliced thin or chopped
1 teaspoon lime zest
¾ cup roasted pine nuts
3 tablespoons fresh cilantro, finely chopped

Wash beets and trim green off the tops. Place in the cooking pot with 1¼ cups water. Lock lid in place; select High Pressure and 30 minutes cooking time. When beep sounds, turn off cooker and use a natural pressure release for 5–8 minutes until all remaining pressure is released. When valve drops, carefully remove lid.

Remove beets from cooker and, when cool enough to handle, rub off skins with paper towel or dish towel and cut into ½-inch wedges.

While beets are cooling, increase the heat to the Brown/Sauté function. Reduce the liquid by half, cooking for 5–6 minutes. Add vinegar and sugar, then return to boil and cook, stirring constantly with heat-resistant spatula, until spatula leaves wide trail when dragged through glaze, 1–2 minutes. Turn off heat.

Add beets and shallot, lime zest, and salt and pepper to taste. Toss in glaze to coat. Transfer beets to serving dish, sprinkle with pine nuts and cilantro, and serve.

Parmesan Risotto

2 tablespoons butter
1 onion, finely chopped
2 garlic cloves, minced
1½ cups arborio rice
½ cup white wine
2 tablespoons cognac
4 cups chicken broth
¾ cup Parmesan cheese, grated

Heat cooking pot on Brown/Sauté function and melt butter. Add onions and cook until softened, about 5 minutes. Stir in garlic and cook another minute.

Stir in rice and toast lightly, about 3-5 minutes. Stir in wine and cognac and cook until almost evaporated, about 1 minute. Stir in 3¼ cups broth.

Lock lid in place; select High Pressure and 6 minutes cooking time. When beep sounds, turn off cooker and use a natural pressure release for 5-6 minutes until all remaining pressure is released. When valve drops, carefully remove lid.

At this point risotto still may look watery, but continue to stir. Turn on Brown/Sauté function and add the cheese. Stir 5-7 minutes until liquid has become thickened. If it becomes too thick, add in remaining stock.

Parmesan Risotto

Robust Goat Cheese Mashed Potatoes

Robust Goat Cheese Mashed Potatoes

2 pounds russet potatoes, roughly cut into 1-inch cubes

3 cloves garlic, peeled

3 scallions, whole

2 sprigs fresh thyme

1 cup chicken broth

¾ cup heavy cream

5 ounces goat cheese

1 teaspoon salt

½ teaspoon pepper

Place the potatoes, garlic, whole scallions, thyme sprigs, and chicken broth in the cooking pot.

Lock lid in place; select High Pressure and 30 minutes cooking time. When beep sounds, turn off cooker and use a natural pressure release for 5-8 minutes until all remaining pressure is released. When valve drops, carefully remove lid.

Drain potatoes into a colander and discard the liquid. Place the potatoes in a large mixing bowl. Discard the scallions and thyme sprig that were cooked under pressure.

Add in the heavy cream, goat cheese, salt, and pepper, and mash together. Serve hot.

Chicken Stock

1 tablespoon vegetable oil

3 pounds chicken, cut into pieces

1 onion, roughly chopped

1 celery stalk, roughly chopped

1 carrot, roughly chopped

1 (1½-inch) ginger root, roughly sliced

3 garlic cloves, roughly chopped

1 teaspoon salt

3 bay leaves

12 cups water

Heat oil in cooking pot on Brown/Sauté function. Brown half of chicken on all sides, about 6–8 minutes; transfer to platter. Repeat with remaining chicken.

In the cooking pot, add onion, celery, and carrot. Cook until softened, about 8–10 minutes. Stir in garlic and ginger and cook for 1 minute.

Add chicken, salt, bay leaves, and water into the pot.

Lock lid in place; select High Pressure and 1 hour cooking time. When beep sounds, turn off cooker and use a natural pressure release for 5–8 minutes until all remaining pressure is released. When valve drops, carefully remove lid.

Strain broth through fine-mesh strainer into clean container, pressing on solids to extract as much liquid as possible; discard solids. Using large spoon, skim excess fat from surface of broth.

Broth can be refrigerated for up to 2 days, or frozen for several months.

Chicken Stock

Balsamic and Honey Pulled Pork

Balsamic and Honey Pulled Pork

1 (2-3 pound) boneless pork shoulder roast

½ cup chicken broth

1 small yellow onion, chopped

½ teaspoon dried thyme

½ teaspoon dried rosemary

1 cup balsamic vinegar

¾ cup ketchup

⅓ cup honey

¼ cup dark brown sugar, packed

1 tablespoon Worcestershire sauce

1 tablespoon Dijon-style mustard

2 cloves garlic, minced

hamburger buns

coleslaw (optional)

Trim fat from pork roast then place in cooking pot and pour broth over top. Add the onions, thyme, and rosemary and lightly sprinkle with pepper.

Cover and set to Slow Cook function on Low setting for 8-9 hours, or High setting for 4½ hours.

During last 30 minutes of roast cooking, in a medium saucepan whisk together balsamic vinegar, ketchup, honey, brown sugar, worcestershire, mustard, garlic, salt and pepper to taste. Bring the sauce to a boil over medium heat, then reduce to a simmer and cook, stirring occasionally, until slightly thickened, about 20-25 minutes.

Remove pork from cooker, shred, and remove any excess fat. Drain onions and broth from cooker and discard. Return shredded pork to cooker and set cooker to Warm setting. Pour in balsamic sauce mixture and toss to evenly coat. Serve on buns with coleslaw if desired.

Braised Chicken Pappardelle

- 1 chicken, about 3½ pounds, cut into pieces
- 1 cup flour
- 1 tablespoon butter
- 1 tablespoon olive oil
- 1 yellow onion, finely chopped
- 2 carrots, peeled and finely chopped
- 3 bay leaves
- 1 celery stalk, finely chopped
- ¾ cup dry white wine
- ¾ cup chicken stock
- ⅔ cup heavy cream
- grated zest of 1 lemon
- juice of ½ lemon
- 1 teaspoon fresh rosemary, coarsely chopped
- 2 teaspoons fresh thyme, coarsely chopped
- 1 pound dried pappardelle
- ⅓ cup Parmesan cheese, grated

In a deep dish plate, evenly coat the chicken in flour, shaking off excess. Set the chicken aside.

Heat your cooking pot on the Brown/Sauté function, melt the butter with the olive oil. Working in batches, add the chicken and sear, turning as needed, until golden brown, about 8–12 minutes total. Transfer the chicken to a plate.

Add the onion, carrots, bay leaves, and celery and sauté until softened and golden, about 5–7 minutes. Pour in the wine and stock.

Lock lid into place; select High Pressure and 35 minutes cooking time. When beep sounds, turn off cooker and use a natural pressure release for 5–8 minutes until all pressure is released. When valve drops, carefully remove lid and set chicken aside to cool.

Bring liquid to a simmer using Brown/Sauté function and cook down the liquid, about 10 minutes. While the broth is simmering, shred chicken, removing and discarding the skin and bones. Set aside.

Remove the bay leaves from the liquid and discard. Cook for 5–8 minutes, then whisk in the cream, salt and pepper to taste. Return to a simmer and cook until reduced slightly, about 5 more minutes. Stir in the lemon zest, lemon juice, rosemary, thyme, and chicken. Heat until warmed through.

Cook the pappardelle until al dente, according to the package directions. Drain, transfer to a warmed serving bowl and add the sauce. Toss to coat evenly. Sprinkle with Parmesan cheese.

Classic Bolognese Sauce

Classic Bolognese Sauce

- 3 tablespoons butter
- ½ onion, finely chopped
- 1 carrot, peeled and finely chopped
- 1 stalk celery, finely chopped
- 3 cloves garlic, minced
- 3 tablespoons tomato paste
- 1½ pounds ground pork
- 1½ pounds ground beef
- 1 teaspoon salt
- ½ teaspoon pepper
- 3 cups whole milk
- 1½ cups red wine
- 3 cups dry white wine
- 2 (28-ounce) cans whole tomatoes, blended in blender or processor until smooth
- ½ teaspoon red pepper flakes, optional
- 1 teaspoon fresh thyme, chopped

Heat cooking pot on Brown/Sauté function, melt butter until bubbling. Add onion, carrot, and celery and cook until softened, about 5-7 minutes. Add garlic and tomato paste and cook about 1 minute. Add meat, 1 teaspoon salt, and ½ teaspoon pepper and cook, breaking up meat, until crumbled into tiny pieces and lightly browned, about 5-8 minutes.

Add milk, bring to vigorous simmer, and cook until milk evaporates, 10 to 15 minutes. Add wines, tomatoes, red pepper flakes, and thyme; cover and bring to boil.

Once mixture comes to boil, reduce to Slow Cooker function on Low setting and simmer until sauce is very thick, about 7-8 hours. Season with salt and pepper and serve.

French Beef Short Ribs

French Beef Short Ribs

- 3 tablespoons butter
- ½ cup flour
- 6 beef short ribs (about 3¼ pounds)
- 1 small yellow onion, finely chopped
- 2 cloves garlic, minced
- 1 tablespoon fresh thyme leaves
- 1 celery stalk, roughly chopped
- 1 carrot, roughly chopped
- 1 bay leaf
- 1 cup red wine
- 1 cup beef broth
- 1 (15-ounce) can whole tomatoes
- 2 tablespoons cornstarch
- ¼ cup water

Heat cooking pot on Brown/Sauté function and melt the butter. Place flour in a shallow dish. Season beef with salt and pepper, then coat in flour, shaking off excess. Add beef to cooker and cook until browned on all sides, about 8 minutes. (Brown beef in batches, if necessary.) Transfer to a plate.

Add onion, garlic, thyme, celery, carrot, and bay leaf to cooker and sauté until soft, about 5 minutes. Add red wine, broth, and tomatoes and return beef to cooker.

Lock lid in place; select High Pressure and 50 minutes cooking time. When beep sounds, turn off cooker and use a natural pressure release for 5–8 minutes until all remaining pressure is released. When valve drops, carefully remove lid.

Transfer meat to a bowl. Strain broth and vegetables with a fine mesh sieve. Add liquid back into the cooking pot. Whisk together the cornstarch and water; add to broth. Select Brown/Sauté function and stir until broth thickens.

Serve short ribs over mashed potatoes, rice, or risotto, and drizzle with finished cooking liquid.

Garlic Ginger Beef with Broccoli

1½ lbs boneless beef chuck roast, well trimmed and sliced into thin strips

1 teaspoon olive oil

1 medium onion, finely chopped

4 cloves garlic, minced

¾ cup beef broth

½ cup soy sauce

⅓ cup brown sugar

3 tablespoons sesame oil

½ teaspoon red pepper flakes

1 pound broccoli florets

4 tablespoons cornstarch

4 tablespoons water

Season beef with salt and pepper. Heat oil in cooking pot on Brown/ Sauté function. When oil begins to sizzle, brown meat in batches until all meat is browned. Transfer meat to a plate.

Add chopped onion, sauté for 1-2 minutes until onion starts to soften. Add garlic and stir for 1 minute more.

Add beef broth, soy sauce, brown sugar, sesame oil, and red pepper flakes to the pot. Stir and heat for another 2 minutes. Add browned beef and juices to the pot

Lock lid in place; select High Pressure and 15 minutes cooking time. When beep sounds, turn off cooker and use a natural pressure release for 5-8 minutes until all remaining pressure is released. When valve drops, carefully remove lid.

Place broccoli in microwave-safe bowl with ¼ cup water. Microwave 3-4 minutes until broccoli is tender.

In a cup combine cornstarch and water; stir until smooth. Add to cooking pot. Stir well to combine. Select Brown/Sauté function and stir until sauce comes to a boil and thickens. Add steamed broccoli.

Serve over hot cooked rice.

Garlic Ginger Beef with Broccoli

Lasagna Tower Stack

Lasagna Tower Stack

2 (9-ounce) packages lasagna noodles (use a premium brand of noodles or they will not hold up. We used Barilla Oven Ready 9-ounce box)

2 tablespoons olive oil

14½ ounces canned whole tomatoes

2 pounds hot and mild beef sausages (use one pound each or all mild/hot)

3 teaspoons Italian seasoning

3 tablespoons flour

3 tablespoons dry milk powder

1 eggplant, sliced on mandoline

1 zucchini, sliced lengthwise on mandoline

2 portobello mushroom caps sliced

4 ounces part-skim mozzarella, grated

2 cups spaghetti sauce (or prepared Bolognese sauce) for serving

Put the noodles in a 9×13-inch dish with 2 tablespoons of olive oil. Pour enough hot water over to cover. Set aside for 20 minutes or until pliable. Drain the noodles, separate them, and set aside.

Depending on the size of your cooking pot, use 4–6 noodles, putting them in a row around the inside walls and then covering the bottom. Overlap the noodles slightly and press against the sides so they stick. On the sides, just do one row and you can add as you fill the pot up.

Crush ⅓ of tomatoes with your hand into the bottom, spread evenly on top of the noodles.

Cover with ⅓ of the sausage and then sprinkle 1 teaspoon of the italian seasoning, 1 tablespoon of flour, and 1 tablespoon dry milk over the layer. Layer ⅓ of the eggplant, zucchini, and mushrooms in layers.

Add ¼ of the remaining noodles in a layer, cut to fit any gaps, slightly overlapping the pieces. Gently press down on the noodles before building the next layer.

Repeat the layers two more times starting with the tomatoes.

Spread the tomato juice from the can on the top of the last layer of noodles.

Set to Slow Cook function on Low setting for 4 hours, or until a knife easily slides through the layers. Turn off the cooker, top with the cheese, cover, and let sit for 20 minutes before serving.

Slice and serve with warmed Bolognese sauce.

Traditional Pozole

2 tablespoons vegetable oil

1¼ pounds boneless pork shoulder, trimmed and cut into 4-inch pieces

1 medium white onion, chopped

5 garlic cloves, minced

1 teaspoon ancho pepper chili powder

1½ tablespoons chili powder

4 cups chicken broth

2 tablespoons cornstarch

4 tablespoons water

1 (29-ounce) can hominy, drained and rinsed

1 avocado, cubed

2 limes, quartered

4 tablespoons cilantro, chopped

Select Brown/Sauté function and add 1 tablespoon oil to the cooking pot. Season pork with salt. Add the pork to the hot oil in the cooking pot and cook until pieces are browned on all sides. When browned, remove to a large bowl.

Add 1 more tablespoon oil to the cooking pot. When hot, add the onion, garlic, and chili powders and sauté until soft, about 5 minutes.

Add broth and pork to cooking pot. Lock lid in place; select High Pressure and 30 minutes cooking time. When beep sounds, turn off cooker and use a natural pressure release for 5–8 minutes until all remaining pressure is released. When valve drops, carefully remove lid.

Remove pork from cooking pot and using two forks, shred pork.

Whisk together corn starch and cold water; add to broth in cooking pot. Select Brown/Sauté function and stir until broth thickens. Stir in shredded pork and hominy. Season with salt and pepper to taste.

Serve with avocado, lime, and cilantro.

Traditional Pozole

Springtime Irish Stew

Springtime Irish Stew

3 pounds boneless lamb shoulder, cut into 2-inch cubes

2 tablespoons olive oil

1 tablespoon butter

2 leeks, cleaned and white portion diced

1 fresh sprig thyme

1 fresh sprig rosemary

1 fresh bay leaf

2 cups beef broth

1 pound red potatoes

4 large carrots, cut into 1-inch pieces

1 cup frozen peas, thawed

2 tablespoons apple cider vinegar

2 teaspoons dried dill weed

Pat lamb dry with paper towels and season lightly all over with salt and pepper. In cooking pot, warm the oil on Brown/Sauté function. Working in batches, brown the meat on each side. Transfer to a plate.

Add the butter and leeks to the pot and cook, stirring occasionally, until softened, about 3 minutes. Add the thyme, rosemary, bay leaf, and broth to the pot. Stir to combine and then return the meat and juices to the pot.

Lock lid into place; select High Pressure for 15 minutes cooking time. When beep sounds, turn off cooker and use a natural pressure release for 5–8 minutes until all remaining pressure is released. When valve drops, carefully remove lid.

Meanwhile, cut the potatoes into quarters. Peel the carrots and cut them into chunks about the same thickness as the potatoes.

Discard the herbs. Put the potatoes and the carrots on top. Do not stir at this point.

Lock lid in place. Cook on High Pressure for 5 minutes. Do a quick pressure release to release any remaining pressure. When valve drops, carefully remove lid.

Stir the peas, vinegar, and dill into the pot.

Turn the pot on to a simmer or Brown/Sauté function until bringing the stew to a simmer or until the peas are heated through, about 2 to 3 minutes.

Pork and Ginger Ramen

3 pounds pork shoulder, cut into equal pieces that are 3-4 inches thick

1 yellow onion, chopped

6 cloves garlic, chopped

5 tablespoons fresh ginger, fresh, peeled and chopped

1 leek, halved, cleaned and chopped

½ pound button mushrooms, brushed clean and coarsely sliced

6 cups chicken broth

2 cups beef broth

1½ pounds fresh ramen noodles

Toppings for Soup

4 eggs, soft boiled

bean sprouts, to taste

4 green onions, finely sliced

sesame oil, to taste

chili oil, to taste

soy sauce, to taste

Season pork with salt and pepper. Heat cooking pot on Brown/ Sauté function and brown the pork on each side. Transfer to a plate and set aside.

Add the yellow onion and stir until browned, about 5 minutes. Stir in the garlic, ginger, leek, mushrooms, and broths. Stir to combine. Add back in pork. Cover and set to Slow Cook function on Low setting for 8 hours.

Transfer the pork to a cutting board. Using 2 forks, break the pork into bite-size chunks. Using a large spoon, skim off and discard any fat from the surface of the broth. Return the pork to the cooking pot. Cover and warm on the Brown/Sauté function until warmed through.

Cook the ramen noodles according to the package directions. Divide the noodles evenly among individual bowls. Ladle the broth and pork over the noodles, dividing them evenly.

Toppings for Soup

Top each bowl with halved soft-boiled egg, bean sprouts, green onion, sesame and chili oil, and soy sauce and serve right away.

Pork and Ginger Ramen

Minestrone Soup

Minestrone Soup

- 1 cup dried medium-sized white beans, rinsed
- 3 tablespoons extra-virgin olive oil
- 2 onions, chopped
- 3 carrots, cut into ¼-inch pieces
- 6 garlic cloves, minced
- 1 (28-ounce) can whole peeled tomatoes
- 4 cups chicken broth
- 4 cups vegetable broth
- 3 cups water
- 2 cups fresh basil, chopped
- 1 teaspoon dried oregano
- 2 medium zucchini, quartered and chopped into ½-inch pieces
- 1 bunch swiss chard, stems removed and roughly chopped
- ½ cup Anelli (or other small soup pasta)
- Parmesan cheese, freshly grated

In the cooking pot on the Brown/Sauté Function, add the beans and cover by 1 inch water. Cook beans until they are just beginning to soften, about 20 minutes. Drain beans and set aside.

In cooking pot, heat 3 tablespoons oil on the Brown/Sauté function. Add onions and carrots and cook until softened, about 5 minutes. Stir in garlic and cook until fragrant, about 30 seconds.

Add tomatoes and juice and cook until most of the liquid is reduced and the pan is nearly dry, about 8-12 minutes.

Stir in broths, water, ½ cup basil, and oregano and bring to boil. Add the beans back into the pot. Cover and set to Slow Cook function on Low setting until beans are tender, 6-7 hours (or cook on High setting, 5-6 hours).

Stir zucchini, chard, and pasta into cooking pot. Cover and cook on Brown/Sauté function until pasta is tender, 20-30 minutes. Stir in remaining basil and top with Parmesan.

Hot Fudge Cake

1 tablespoon butter, room temperature, for greasing

3 eggs

1½ sticks butter, melted

1½ cups sugar

⅔ cup unsweetened cocoa powder

⅓ cup flour

1 teaspoon vanilla extract

½ teaspoon salt

½ cup semisweet chocolate, broken into pieces

vanilla ice cream

Line the cooking pot with a piece of foil, then grease the foil with 1 tablespoon of butter. Set aside.

Slightly beat the eggs until mixed together. In a separate bowl, stir together the melted butter, sugar, cocoa powder, flour, eggs, vanilla, and ½ teaspoon salt. Sprinkle in the chocolate chunks and stir until chocolate is just mixed into the batter.

Transfer the batter into the foil-lined cooking pot. Cover and set to Slow Cook function on Low setting for 3 hours. The cake should be set around the edges and gooey in the center.

Serve the cake warm, spooned into a bowl and topped with ice cream.

Rice Pudding

Rice Pudding

1 cup rice

1 cup water

2 cups heavy cream, divided

⅛ teaspoon salt

½ cup sugar

½ vanilla bean, sliced lengthwise

½ teaspoon cardamom (optional)

½ teaspoon vanilla extract

¾ cup raisins

In cooking pot, combine rice, water, ½ cup cream, and salt.

Lock lid into place; select High Pressure for 5 minutes cooking time. When beep sounds turn off cooker and use a natural pressure release for 7–10 minutes until all remaining pressure is released. When valve drops, carefully remove lid.

Add 1½ cups cream and sugar to rice in cooking pot. Stir to combine.

Scrape in vanilla bean and add cardamom (optional) and vanilla extract to mixture. Select Brown/Sauté function and cook, stirring constantly, until mixture starts to boil. Turn off cooker. Remove cooking pot from the cooker.

Stir in raisins. The pudding will still seem a little loose and watery, but it will thicken as it cools. Remove the vanilla bean.

Served topped with whipped cream, and a sprinkle of cinnamon or nutmeg, if desired.

Key Lime Pie

Crust

¾ cup graham cracker crumbs

4 tablespoons unsalted butter, melted

1 tablespoon sugar

Filling

4 large egg yolks

1 (14-ounce) can sweetened condensed milk

½ cup key lime juice, freshly squeezed

⅓ cup sour cream

2 tablespoons grated key lime zest

Crust
In a small 1-quart pyrex glass bowl that will fit inside your cooking pot (or you can use individual silicone cups), combine the graham cracker crumbs, butter, and sugar. Press evenly in the bottom and up the sides of the pan. Place in the freezer for 10 minutes.

Filling
In a large mixing bowl, beat the egg yolks until they are light yellow. Gradually beat in sweetened condensed milk until thickened. Gradually add lime juice and beat until smooth. Stir in sour cream and zest. Pour batter into the baking dish on top of the crust. Cover top of dish with aluminum foil.

Pour 1 cup of water into the cooking pot. Carefully lower your pie into the cooking pot.

Lock lid into place; select High Pressure for 20 minutes cooking time. When beep sounds, turn off cooker and use a natural pressure release 8–10 minutes until all remaining pressure is released. When valve drops, carefully remove lid.

Remove pie and check to see if the middle is set. If not, cook an additional 5 minutes using same settings as above but use less cook time.

Remove the baking dish to cool. Remove aluminum foil. When pie is cooled, refrigerate covered with plastic wrap for at least 4 hours.

Key Lime Pie

About the Author

Allison Waggoner, acclaimed television host, seen in more than 80 million homes, has recorded more than 80,000 hours of LIVE television, which is more than Oprah and Jay Leno combined! You can see Allison in the kitchen with celebrities, such as Chefs Todd English, Andrew Zimmern, Paula Deen, Bobby Deen, Jamie Deen, Kevin Dundon, the Beekman Boys, and Captain Sig Hanson. You've seen her on The Food Network's *Unwrapped*, and you can currently join in with her on *Evine Live*. Just in case you didn't know her true passion, it's FOOD and sharing it with YOU! As a classically trained chef, Allison's culinary and marketing career brought her to the attention of television executives. She first appeared as a guest host, bringing her confections and family culinary history to the home shopping world.

Growing up in the chocolate industry inspired a journey filled with delicious and innovative cuisine. Allison started with her family's gourmet chocolates, creating some of the finest award-winning confections in the world. Her culinary designs have been featured in Crate & Barrel, Culinary Product Magazine, Ghirardelli Chocolate Company, Godiva Chocolatier, Walt Disney World, Fancy Food

Magazine, Target, Universal Studios, Williams-Sonoma, and on The Food Network.

Her In the Kitchen cookbook series began with *A Collection of Home and Family Memories*, released in 2014. Her second book, *A Gathering of Friends*, is a nostalgic collection of recipes to celebrate the moments in our lives and is filled with simple, delicious dishes for every day of the week. Added to her collection is *Air Fryer Cookbook*, the #1 bestselling air fryer book in the country, including a newly released updated edition.

Alison lives in the Twin Cities, Minnesota.

Visit her at www.allisonwaggoner.com

0 26575 19288 9